SHEILA KIMONO STYLE

シーラの着物スタイル

シーラ・クリフ　撮影：タッド・フォング

sheila cliffe photographer: Todd Fong

かもめの本棚

はじめに

　大学で教えるときも、ちょっとお出かけをするときも、友人に会うときも、ほぼ毎日、着物姿で暮らしている私を見て、「どうして着物がそんなに好きなのですか？」と声をかける人がいます。そんなとき、私は必ず次のような質問を返すことにしています。「話を聞いてもらえる時間が、どれくらいありますか？」。なぜなら、私が着物を愛する理由はあまりにもたくさんあって、ひとことではとても答えられないからです。

　今から30年以上前にイギリスから来日し、初めて着物を目にしたとき、艶やかな絹の光沢と、型染め・手描き・織りなどの技法を駆使したデザイン性豊かな模様や柄に、一瞬にして心を奪われてしまいました。その美しさは私の感性を刺激し、虜にしてしまったのです。その後、着物の歴史や文化、技法などを学んでいくにつれて、着物が代々引き継がれていく"家族の歴史"を物語っていると知り、もっともっと好きになりました。

　着物は軽々と時代をこえることができます。たとえば100年前の洋服を現代人が着ると、コスプレに間違われるか、ちょっと変わった人に思われてしまうかもしれません。ところが100年前の着物で街を歩いても、少しも変ではありません。この違いは何か？　それは、100年前の着物も現代の着物も基本の形は全く同じだからです。模様や柄、素材、技法は流行に応じて変化したとしても、長方形の布を縫い合わせたシンプルなシルエットは昔も今も変わりません。

　もう一つの理由として、着物は洋服のように完成された存在ではないことが挙げられると思います。アクセサリーを少し足すことはありますが、着るだけでほぼ完成形となる洋服に対し、着物は素材、すなわちキャンバスです。どのような帯や小物をプラスするかによって、同じ着物でも何通りもの着こなしが可能になります。自分だけの装いを組み立てられるのも着物の魅力であり、そのプロセスもまた、着物を着る楽しみの一つ。時代や流行の変化にも柔軟に対応することができるのです。だからこそ同じ着物が何十年もの間、親から子へ、人から人へと受け継がれてきたのでしょう。

私は100枚以上の着物を持っていますが、そのほとんどが骨董市や古着屋、インターネットなどで見つけた数千円クラスの古着やアンティークです。中には丈が短いものや、着物としての役目を終えてリメーク用の布地として売られていたものもあります。でも心から気に入った着物と出会ったら、サイズや汚れはあまり気になりません。そこから湧いてくるインスピレーションを大切にして、一度でいいから自分ならではの着こなしをしたいと願うのです。そして、それを写真に収めることで、もう一度その着物本来の美しさを皆に見せたい。古い着物の物語の中にもう一つのエピソードを加えたいと思うのです。

　英語で「A picture is worth a thousand words.（1枚の絵は1000の言葉に値する）」ということわざありますが、何千もの言葉を尽くしても、着物の魅力を十二分に伝えることはできません。それこそが、この写真集をつくろうと思ったいちばんの理由です。

　ここで紹介した写真は、着物研究家である私の活動を日ごろから手伝ってくれている写真家のタッド・フォングさんが、2017年から1年間にわたって撮り続けたものです。一部の例外はあるものの、撮影地は私の住まいや勤務地である大学のキャンパス周辺がほとんど。普段から慣れ親しんでいる場所で、私服の着物コーディネートを撮影しました。1冊にまとめたことで、四季折々の移ろいを装いで演出するという、着物ならではの特徴も見えてくることでしょう。

　とはいえ、モデルである私自身は背が低くて横幅がある体型ですし、年齢を重ねた顔には皺もたくさんあり、一般的なモデルとはまるで異なる見た目です。ところが、着物を羽織るだけでこれらの欠点は全部隠され、エレガンスに、かわいらしく、そして女性らしく変身できる。不思議と自分に自信が持てるようになるのです。これもまた着物のよさ、すなわち魔法なのではないでしょうか。
　私の1年間の着物スタイルが皆さんの感性を刺激し、着物の美しさと可能性を再発見する機会になることを願っています。

Introduction

Because I'm wearing kimono almost everyday, to teach at my university, going to events, and when going out with friends, sometimes people ask me, "What is it about kimono that you love that much?" I usually reply with another question. "How long do you have to listen to my explanation?" The reason for this is that there are so many reasons why I love kimono, that it would be impossible to give a short answer to the question.

When I came to Japan over thirty years ago and I saw kimono for the first time, I fell in love with the lustrous glossy silk, the stencil dyeing, hand painting, the weaving, and the richness and variety of patterns and designs. It stole my heart. It was later that I learned about kimono culture, about the complex processes in making it, and about kimono being passed down from generation to generation, speaking of family history. Then I fell even deeper in love.

Kimono can easily cross generations. Suppose someone today wore a dress that was a hundred years old. People would either think it was a kind of cos-play, or they would think that person was a little strange in the head. So what is that difference between western clothes and kimono? Well, one reason is that kimono has not changed in shape in the last one hundred years. Only the patterns and designs, the cloth and the decorative techniques have changed. The use of one long narrow piece of cloth is just the same now as it was in the past.

There is another reason. I think that kimono, unlike most western dresses, are not finished items. Although they can be altered a little with accessories, the dress is the finished look, whereas the kimono is the raw material, the canvas if you like. Depending on how one coordinates it, what obi and accessories one brings to it, with the same kimono it is possible to produce many different looks. Being able to produce one's own looks is one of the strengths of kimono, and the dressing process is one of the joys of wearing it. Being able to subtly incorporate the old in fashionable new ways is really exciting, and is one of the reasons why mothers can pass kimono on to their children and it can work years and years later, and why it can be given from person to person.

I have over a hundred kimono, but they are mostly from antique, second hand kimono shops, or from used kimono internet shops, and most cost only a few thousand yen. In my collection are those that are really too short for me, and those that are really worn out and being sold as material for remaking into something else. But if I see a kimono and I really love it, I will buy it in spite of it being the wrong size, or having some stains. The inspiration that I get about how it could look when worn, is more important to me. I really want to wear it again my way, and show its beauty. Then if I can take a photograph of it, I can show everyone its beauty. Even if I can only do it once, I want to create one more chapter in the life of that old kimono.

In English there is a well-known saying, a picture paints a thousand words. But I think that you can speak thousands of words, without being able to express the beauty of kimono. That is the main reason why I decided to make this photo book. The photographs here were taken by my friend Todd Fong, who is working with me photographing my kimono research project. They were taken throughout the year 2017. With a few exceptions the photographs were taken in my neighborhood or near my university. They're places I know well, and I took them wearing my own kimono coordinations. Because they are collected into a book, it is possible to see the changing of the seasons in the scenes and clothing, which is another special aspect of kimono style.

I am nothing like model material. I am too short and rather wide, too old with many wrinkles. You would not pick me to show off your clothing. But just by wrapping kimono around me, it hides my failings, and enables me to create elegant, cute or feminine images. It's strange but knowing I can do that gives me confidence in my style. It's a magical strength of kimono.
I am hoping that this collection will inspire you, and be an opportunity for you to reconsider the beauty and possibilities of kimono.

I wore a celebratory pine,
bamboo and plum blossom yuzen kimono
for my first visit to the shrine.
The pokkuri came
from a second hand shop.

おめでたい松竹梅の友禅の着物を着て初詣へ。
ぽっくりは古着屋で見つけました。

南天といえばお正月に飾るものですが、その赤い実を見て私が思い出すのはクリスマスホーリー（西洋ヒイラギ）。この着物の柄も、どことなくヒイラギの葉に似ているでしょ。

Heavenly bamboo, (nanten) is a New Year decoration, but the red berries always remind me of the holly we used to display at Christmas. This design looks like holly to me.

縦縞と花模様の組み合わせに遊び心を感じる大正時代の「散歩着」。
A slightly playful image is given by the combination of stripes and flowers together in this Taisho period walking out wear.

牡丹と薔薇のぼかし染めの色留袖に、孔雀の帯を合わせてエレガントに。自前の髪で日本髪を結ってみました。

An elegant look with beautifully shaded peonies and roses on this iro tomesode, which I combined with a peacock obi. I used my own hair to make this nihongami Japanese hair style.

011

I wore this obi because 2017 was the Year of the Rooster. snowflakes are the pattern on this kimono, which I wore very short to go with my boots. I'll be fine, even walking in the snow!

この写真は2017年の酉年に撮影したもの。
雪の結晶をモチーフにした雪輪文様の着物を短めに着て、
長靴を履けば、雪の日のお出かけもへっちゃら！

私の
いちばん好
きな緑色の着物だ
から、少しくらいサイズ
が小さくても平気。腕が隠
れるショールと、動きのある
イアリングでごまかし
ちゃいます。

This kimono is my favorite shade of green, so I'm not bothered that it's actually rather small. I'm faking it by covering up with a shawl and using some dangly earrings.

白いシャツに端切れでつくった蝶ネクタイ、
靴ひもの帯締めとスニーカー。
これも私流の着物スタイル。
バッグも傘も自転車も
すべて桜と同じピンク色。
頭に乗せた小さな帽子も
お気に入り。

I'm wearing a white shirt with a bow tie
I made from old kimono cloth,
shoe laces for obi jime and sneakers.
It's my kimono style.
My bag, umbrella and bike are all pink
like the blossoms
and I have a tiny straw hat
on my head.

モダンガールが登場した大正・昭和初期の着物は、柄が斬新で色鮮やか。帽子との愛称もGood！
The modern girls appeared in the Taisho and early Showa periods, (1910s-1930s) wearing bold designs in bright colors. The hat goes well with the kimono. It's good!

*Red wisteria and a huge butterfly
adorn this kimono, and
I have added a fringed beaded bag
to go with it.*

赤い藤の花と蝶が大胆に意匠化された着物には、
フリンジが揺れる黒のビーズバッグを斜めがけ。

撮影地は、なんと近所の野菜スタンド！
巨大なトマトの向こう側で旬の採れたて野菜を販売中！
Amazingly, I took this photo against a local vegetable stand.
On the other side of the giant tomato is a shelf with veggies for sale!

暑い日は襦袢を着けずに、着物1枚と兵児帯だけでラフに過ごしたい。
On hot days I just like to hang out with a single layer of kimono and a heko obi.

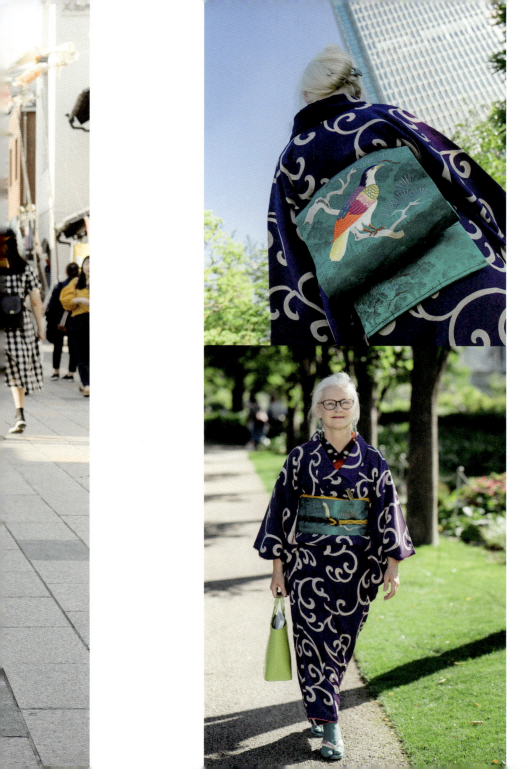

ここは
伊豆半島ですが、
気分はまるで
地中海！

In reality it's Izu Peninsula, in my imagination, the Med!

海沿いの町、伊豆・下田に黒船がやって来たのは今から160年以上も前のこと。
黒船来航をイメージして、帆船柄の帯をセレクトしました。
It was 160 years ago that the black ships first arrived at the seaside town of shimoda, Izu.
Thinking of that arrival, I chose an obi with a black galleon.

着物は私の"日本の先生"

　初めて日本に来たのは24歳のとき。大学の夏休みを利用した短期旅行のつもりでしたが、骨董市で見た華やかな着物に魅せられて、そのまま30年以上も日本に住み続けています。最初に買ったのは赤い長襦袢。それを友人に見せたら「これは下着だよ」と言われてびっくり。「こんなに美しいものを中に着るの？」という驚きと同時に、着物の世界に引き込まれていきました。

　日本で暮らすと決めてからは着付けの学校に2年間通い、趣味で染め物にも挑戦。何度も着物屋さんに通って質問したり、着物雑誌をめくったり。最初は全く話せなかった日本語も、そんなことを繰り返すうちに自然と覚えてしまいました。来日以来、私の生活の一部にはずっと着物があります。着物は私の住み家だし、日本のことを教えてくれた先生。今では大学教授として着物に関する研究を続けながら、その魅力を国内外に広めることがライフワークとなっています。

Kimono, Teacher of Japan

I first came to Japan when I was 24. I was making use of the university summer vacation and intended it to be a short trip. However I became so fascinated with the beautiful kimono I had seen at the shrine flea market that I've now been living here for over thirty years. The first item I bought was a red nagajuban. I was so shocked when a friend told me that it was underwear. "You mean you wear this beautiful thing on the inside?" It was such a surprise and I became drawn further into the world of kimono.

When I decided to live and work here, I went to kimono school for two years, I did stencil dyeing as a hobby, and I repeatedly went to kimono shops asking questions, and to book shops, to look at kimono magazines. At first I couldn't speak Japanese at all, but with repeated questioning, I began to learn it naturally. Since I came to Japan, kimono has always been a part of my life, it's a sort of home for me, and it's also my teacher about Japan. Now, as a university professor, kimono is my area of research, and its my lifework to spread knowledge about the kimono both in Japan and in other countries, too.

私は私

　小さいころからおしゃれが大好きでしたが、双子姉妹だったので、いつもママが作ったおそろいの服を着せられていました。双子とはいえ髪の色は違うから区別がつくはずなのに、同じ服を着ているというだけでみんなが私たちの名前を間違える。それが嫌で仕方がなかったですね。その反動なのか、クラスの女の子が全員ミニスカートをはいているのに、一人だけロングスカートで学校へ。でも結局、みんなに笑われて泣いたこともあります。今、考えてみると、"私は私"というメッセージを服装で伝えたかったのだと思います。

　ファッションという観点で捉えると、着物も洋服と同じ。日本の伝統文化である以前に、自分らしさを表現する手段の一つだと思うのです。TPOに応じた和装独特のルールもしっかり学びましたが、それに縛られると自分らしい表現ができなくなると思ったのも事実。だからこそ失礼のないように気をつけながらも、個性を生かした着こなしを楽しんでいます。

I am Me

From my childhood, I liked to dress up, but I am one of twins, so my mother would always make two dresses, and I had to wear the same thing as my sister. Even though I was blonde and my sister had brown hair and our faces were different, everyone mixed us up. I really hated that. As a protest to sameness I once went to school in a dress that had a long hem, when everyone was wearing miniskirts. Of course, I came home in tears after everyone laughed at me. When I look back on it, I was just trying to establish myself through my clothing choices.

From the point of view of fashion, kimono and western clothing are the same. Before kimono is Japanese traditional culture, it is a way of expressing oneself. I have learned the special time, place, occasion, appropriate rules of the kimono system but if one gets completely tied up in those rules, it becomes difficult to fully express oneself. So while being very careful not to make a serious social faux pas, I am enjoying expressing my own style through the kimono.

美しい振り袖をまとうと、気持ちまで若返ります。振り袖を着るのに、年齢制限も、未婚限定というルールもありません。もっと着物を楽しまなくっちゃ！

When you wrap yourself in a beautiful furisode, you feel young again. It's not a rule that only young single women wear furisode. We should have more fun with kimono!

Taking a hint from the carp in splashing water, I used a polka dot obi.
鯉の水しぶきからヒントを得て、帯も水玉模様に。

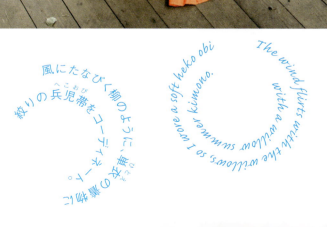

風にたなびく柳のように、兵児帯をコーディネート。絞りの兵児帯を夏着物に。

The wind flirts with a willow so I wore a soft heko obi with a willow summer kimono.

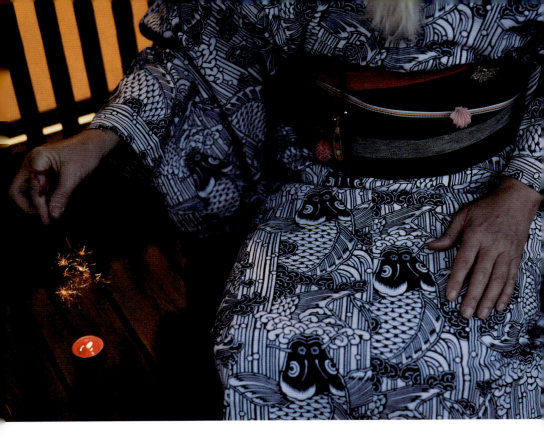

This is a replica of an Edo period stencil on a ro yukata. The large carp design means it was probably designed for a man.

江戸の型染めを再現した絽の浴衣。鯉の模様が大きくてはっきりしているから、もともとは男性用だったのかもしれません。

淡い紫の菖蒲柄にブルーの差し色を効かせた夏の小紋。
星の形をした帯留は友人の手づくりです。
I made this dull purple iris summer komon work by adding a bright blue.
The star obidome was hand-made by a friend.

自宅のデッキでくつろぐときは、スカーフを帯代わりに結んでリラックス。
Relaxing at home on the deck with just a scarf for an obi.

薔薇模様の着物を着ると、故郷のイギリスを思い出します。
When I wear rose patterns, I remember my birthplace, England.

明治の終わりごろの古い絽の着物。しっとり上品に着る夏の礼装です。
A late Meiji ro kimono. Still elegant, summer formal wear.

これがイギリス発の着物パンクファッション！
Punk kimono fashion coming from England!

サマー
ウールの
夕涼みコーデ。
古い木綿の絞りの
帯と薔薇の帯留めが
アクセント。

A cool
summer
wool
kimono.
I coordinated
an old cotton
shibori obi with a
rose obidome as an
accent.

私は"着物のトレンドハンター"

　私は、自分のことを"着物のトレンドハンター"と言っています。着物が芸術品としてではなくファッションとして生き残るためには、流行や人々の暮らしから消費者の潜在的なニーズを把握し、情報を発信することが必要だと考えているからです。

　そんな私が新たに取り組んでいるのが、「箪笥開きプロジェクト」です。友人の石岡久美子さんと写真家のタッド・フォングさんの協力を得て始めたこのプロジェクトの調査対象は、20代から80代の日本人女性50人。彼女たちの自宅に行き、所有している着物の枚数や種類、入手経路や収納方法を調査するだけでなく、お気に入りの着物ストーリーや困っていることなど、所有者の実態とエピソードの聞き取りを続けています。こんなリアルな調査をした人は、今までほとんどいないと思います。50人分の調査が終わったらその分析を進め、いずれは一冊の本にまとめたいと考えています。

Kimono Trend Hunter

I call myself a kimono trend hunter. For kimono to survive as fashion and not as some kind of art object, it is necessary to grasp trends, people's kimono lifestyles, and the needs of kimono end-users. I think its important to spread this information.

In order to do this I started "The Kimono Closet" project. With the help of my friends Kumiko Ishioka and photographer Todd Fong, I am examining the kimono closets of fifty Japanese women from their 20s to their 80s. We go to their homes, count the numbers and types of kimono, note where they came from and how they are stored. In addition we ask participants to tell us their problems with kimono life and the stories of kimono that have special meanings for them. I don't think anyone has done such research on the kimono user before. When we have finished the interviews and examined the data, I think I would like to gather the information into a book.

時代をこえてつながる力

　着物で街を歩いたり、ＳＮＳに着物姿の写真を投稿したりすると、知らない人から「すてきね」と声をかけられることがあります。そんなご縁から、着物を譲ったり、譲られたりすることも。こんなこと、洋服ではあまりないと思いませんか？　東日本大震災の翌年には、津波で家財を流された女性が無事に成人式を迎えられるようにと、私も知人を通じて振り袖を何枚か被災地に送りました。このように、着物には人と人とをつなげる力があります。母から子へと受け継がれた着物を着ることで、時代をこえてたくさんの人とつながる。そして、その作り手や場所ともつながることができるのです。

　初めての人は背伸びをせず、古着やポリエステルといった安価な着物からでも十分です。デニムとハイネックの上にお気に入りの着物を羽織って、足元はブーツ。実はこれ、私が寒い日によくやるコーディネート。こんなふうに最初はハードルを下げて、まずは着物を楽しむことから始めてください。

Power to Cross Generations and Connect People

When I am walking in the street, or when I upload photos on social media, a lot of strangers comment, "That looks so nice" to me. I have even had people donate kimono to me. I don't think that that would ever happen if I was wearing western clothing. The year after the Great East Japan earthquake and tsunami I sent some furisode to the disaster area so that girls who had survived and who had become twenty could celebrate their coming of age. Kimono has the power to connect people. When a mother gives a kimono to her daughter, they become connected across the generations. The maker or the place where the kimono is made is also somehow connected when a buyer chooses and orders a kimono.

For a beginner a small step, such as a used, polyester or denim kimono, is fine. Wear it with a high-necked shirt and boots. It's actually a way of coordination that I'm fond of in cold weather. Lets just keep the bar low so we can see many people starting to enjoy wearing kimono.

着物作家の友人がつくってくれた大切な絵絣。これを着ると手づくりの温もりに包まれます。

A very special handmade picture ikat kimono, made by my friend. When I wear it, I feel the special warmth of handmade items.

この日はちょっと遊び心を出して、表と裏を逆にして帯を締めてみました。意外とステキでしょ？

I was feeling a bit playful, so I put the obi on inside out. Surprisingly fun!

赤！×黒！
RED! × BLACK!

秋の旅路は着物にブーツで。 For an autumn trip, kimono with boots.

*Being able to put all kinds of colours
and patterns together,
is one of the joys of kimono play.
A sword hilt can become
a great obidome.*

色や柄の多彩な組み合わせと枠にはまらない小物づかいが、
着物遊びの魅力。刀の鍔だって帯留になるんだもの。

Kimono柄を身にまとって読書タイム。おそらく昭和初期の着物です。
Reading time in a kimono saying kimono! It's probably from the early Showa period.

着物の下にタートルネックを着るのも私流。温くておすすめです。

*I recommend wearing a turtle neck top under kimono.
Its very warm.*

2枚の着物を重ねて着ました。一度はやってみたかった着こなしです。
I wanted to try wearing two kimono on top of each other.

「縦縞に花柄」は私の大好きなモチーフの一つ。
Stripes with flowers. It's one of the motifs I really like.

厚手のタイツとハイカットの登山靴を履いて、
楽しい雪遊び！

Thick tights and climbing boots.
I'm ready for playing in the snow!

古くて染みもある帯だけれど、
ひと目ぼれで手に入れました。
こんなふうに1点ものとの出会いを
大切にしています。
This obi is old and stained,
but I fell in love with the design,
and I wanted to wear it
at least once!

お気に入りの柄でしたが、生地が傷んで着られなくなってしまいました。でもその前に撮影できたから、この着物は写真の中でまだ生き続けています。

I loved this pattern, but the cloth was really damaged and it can't be worn any more. But before it was retired, I took this photograph, so it still lives on here.

ネックレスやブレスレットをする人もいるけれど、私はイヤリング派。
着物とのバランスを考慮して選んでいます。

Some people wear necklaces or bracelets,
but I think that earrings are the best balanced to go with kimono.

My obi and obidome were given by a participant in my "The Kimono Closet" project. They belonged to her mother. When they are worn, they do not look old and faded at all. She must have been a stylish woman.

帯と帯留は、「簞笥開きプロジェクト」(72ページ参照)でお世話になった女性のお母さまの形見の品。今、身に着けても全く色あせて見えません。きっと、とてもおしゃれな方だったのですね。

Sheila Cliffe（シーラ・クリフ）
1961年イギリス生まれ。リーズ大学大学院博士課程修了。埼玉大学、立教大学の非常勤講師を経て、十文字学園女子大学教授。大学で英語と着物文化を教える傍ら、国内外で着物展覧会やファッションショーの企画・プロデュースをするなど多彩な活動を展開。2002年、民族衣裳文化普及協会「きもの文化普及賞」を受賞。著書に『日本のことを英語で話そう』（中経出版）。17年には、これまでの研究結果をまとめた英語版の著書『The Social Life of Kimono』（Bloomsbury）を出版。クリエーターとして注目を集めるAKIRA TIMES初の写真集『KIMONO times』（リブロアルテ）の出版サポートなど、活動の幅をさらに広げている。

Todd Fong（タッド・フォング）
1969年アメリカ合衆国カリフォルニア州オークランド生まれ。サンノゼ州立大学で映画製作を専攻するが、写真家としてのキャリアを追求するために退学。カリフォルニア、シンガポールに在住後、現在は東京を拠点に活動中。2014年から「箪笥開きプロジェクト」の写真家として、シーラ・クリフの研究をサポートしている。着物以外にも、ポートレート、ファッション、旅行などの撮影経験がある。プライベートではブログの配信や若者を対象にした撮影指導などにも取り組んでいる。

Sheila Cliffe
Born in 1961 in the U.K. Graduated with a Ph.D. from the University of Leeds. After teaching at Saitama and Rikkyo Universities she became a professor at Jumonji Gakuen Women's University. Besides teaching English and Kimono Culture, she works on kimono shows and kimono fashion shows in Japan and other countries. She was awarded The Kimono Spreading award by the The Cultural Foundation for Preserving the National Costume of Japan, in 2002. She has written "Explaining Japan in easy English", (Chukei Publishing) and in 2017 published the results of her kimono research as "The Social Life of Kimono" (Bloomsbury). She supported the publication of creator AKIRA TIMES book "Kimono times" (Libro Arte), and continues to expand her contributions to kimono.

Todd Fong
Born in 1969 in Oakland, California. Attended San Jose State University (California) as a Film major, but left university to pursue a photography career. He has lived and worked in California, Singapore and most recently, Tokyo. He has been working with Sheila Cliffe as a photographer on "The Kimono Closet" project since 2014. Besides photographing kimono, he has done work in portraiture, fashion, and travel photography. In his free time, he enjoys blogging and teaching photography to young people.

おわりに

　本書で紹介した私の着物姿は、約1年間をかけて撮影したものです。忙しい1年でしたが、大好きな着物を箪笥から出し、帯を選び、半襟を縫う、といった準備や、撮影スポットを探して自転車で近所を巡った経験は楽しく、とても充実した時間でした。私の所有している古い着物のことや、身近な町の風景、四季の移り変わりなどを、あらためて見つめ直すきっかけにもなりました。そして、物を大切にする人でいたい、自然を守り続けたいと、これまで以上に強く願うようになりました。今後も、何世代にも渡って愛された古い着物を大切しつつ、自分の住む町の美しさも発見していきたいと思っています。

　撮影を担当してくれた写真家のタッド・フォングさんは、神様が創造した美しい世界を見る目を持ち、愛情あふれる写真を撮ってくれました。タッドさんのひたむきさと情熱がなかったら、この本は存在しなかったことでしょう。人を大切にする優しい彼がいてくれるから、私も着物の研究が続けられますし、この本を世に送り出すことができました。深く感謝します。そして、「かもめの本棚」編集部の村尾由紀編集長、狭間由恵さんにも感謝します。頑張り屋さんの女性たちと一緒に本をつくるのは楽しかったし、私の力にもなりました。このほか、応援してくださったたくさんの方々に感謝しています。本書を手にした皆さまが、少しでも着物に対する興味を持ってくれたらうれしい限りです。

　着物に関する私の研究と情報発信は、これからも続きます。日本の美しい着物文化が次世代へと継承されることを願い、着物や浴衣の着付け体験を通して学生たちに着物の楽しさや文化を伝えるとともに、ファッションショーや講演会などの活動も積極的に展開していく所存です。応援よろしくお願いいたします。

シーラ・クリフ

Afterword

It took about a year to take all the photographs in this book. It was a busy year, but it was very fulfilling. I got out all my favorite kimono from my chests, chose the obi and sewed the collars. I also spent time going around my neighborhood on my bicycle, looking for beautiful places to take the photographs. All this preparation was fun. It was a chance to think about the importance of my old kimono, the beauty of my neighborhood and the changing of the seasons. I want to be mindful of these things.

This book would not have happened if Todd had not continued to take my photograph when we went out. Todd always looks at the beautiful world God made and shoots it full of love. He is a very caring person, and it is because of him that I can continue my research and produce this book, so I am really thankful. I am also very grateful to Kamome no Hondana online magazine editor in chief Murao Yuki, and Hazama Naoe for their hard work editing this project. It has been an amazing experience to work with these two powerhouse women and I am so inspired by them. Thank you to everyone who has encouraged me along the way. To everyone who has bought the book, I hope it will hold some kimono inspiration for you.

My plans are to continue to research and share information about kimono. I hope that kimono culture can continue to the next generation. I will be giving students fun experiences wearing kimono and yukata, and teaching them about kimono, and I will continue to plan fashion shows and presentations. Thank you to all of my supporters out there.

Sheila Cliffe

SHEILA KIMONO STYLE
ーシーラの着物スタイルー

2018年10月29日	第1刷発行
2019年 1 月17日	第2刷発行
2021年11月 1 日	第3刷発行

著　者	シーラ・クリフ　Sheila Cliffe
撮　影	タッド・フォング　Todd Fong (Photographer)
発行者	原田邦彦
発行所	東海教育研究所 〒160-0023　東京都新宿区西新宿7-4-3　升本ビル 電話 03-3227-3700　ファクス 03-3227-3701 eigyo@tokaiedu.co.jp
印刷・製本	株式会社シナノパブリッシングプレス
装丁・本文デザイン	稲葉奏子
編集協力	川島省子

Ⓒ Sheila Cliffe 2018 ／ Printed in Japan
ISBN978-4-924523-00-5 C0077

JCOPY ＜出版者著作権管理機構 委託出版物＞
本書の無断複製は著作権法上での例外を除き禁じられています。複製される場合は、そのつど事前に、出版者著作権管理機構 (電話 03-5244-5088、FAX 03-5244-5089、e-mail: info@jcopy.or.jp) の許諾を得てください。

乱丁・落丁の場合はお取り替えいたします
定価はカバーに表示してあります